I Like Cars

Angela Aylmore

www.raintreepublishers.co.uk
Visit our website to find out
more information about
Raintree books.

To order:

☎ Phone 0845 6044371

🖹 Fax +44 (0) 1865 312263

🖳 Email myorders@capstonepub.co.uk

Customers from outside the UK please telephone +44 1865 312262

First published in Great Britain by Heinemann Library,
Halley Court, Jordan Hill, Oxford OX2 8EJ, part
of Harcourt Education. Heinemann is a registered
trademark of Harcourt Education Ltd.

Editorial: Dan Nunn and Sarah Chappelow
Design: Joanna Hinton-Malivoire
Picture research: Erica Newbery
Production: Duncan Gilbert

Origination: Chroma Graphics (Overseas) Pte. Ltd
Printed and bound in China, China by South
China Printing Co. Ltd.

10-digit ISBN 0 431 10957 5
13-digit ISBN 978 0 431 10957 2
11 10
10 9 8 7 6 5 4 3

British Library Cataloguing in Publication Data
Aylmore, Angela
   I like cars. - (Things I like)
   1. Automobiles - Juvenile literature
   I. Title
   629.2'22
A full catalogue record for this book is available from
the British Library.

Acknowledgements
The publishers would like to thank the following for
permission to reproduce photographs: Alamy pp. **10**
(Mark Scheuer), **16** (Bananastock), **22** (Model T Ford,
Mark Scheuern); Alvey & Towers pp. **6**, **22**; Auto-
Express p. **8**; Corbis pp. **7** (Alan Schein Photography),
9 (Schlegelmilch Photography), **11** (Bettmann), **12**
(Bettmann), **14**, **20–21** (MGM), **22**; Jupiter Images pp.
15 (Bananastock), **17** (Bananastock); Digital Vision pp.
4–5 (red car); Photos.com pp. **4**; Photolink pp. **5** (racing
car); REX Features p. **19** (Tim Rooke); Science Photo
Library pp. **18** (Keith Kent), **22** (Keith Kent); Science
and Society p. **13** (Science Museum).

Cover photograph of a sports car reproduced with
permission of Getty Images (Neil Nissing/Taxi).

Contents

Some words are shown in bold, **like this.** You can find out what they mean by looking in the Glossary.

Cars

I like cars.

I will tell you my favourite things about cars.

Different cars

This car is tiny!

This car is so big that my whole class could fit inside it.

These cars can drive
through water!

This car is my favourite.
It is a racing car. It is
very fast.

Old cars

I like old cars too. I have seen lots of old cars at a car **museum**.

This was one of the
first ever cars.

You had to wind this car up with a handle!

The first cars were very slow. You could run faster than this old car!

Taking care of cars

I like helping my dad to take care of his car. We wash it to keep it clean.

We go to the **petrol** station.
Mum fills the car with petrol.

Sometimes, mum puts air in the **tyres.**

Once our car **broke down.**
We took it to a garage to
be **repaired.**

Famous cars

I like famous cars. This is
the fastest car in the world.
It is called the Thrust SSC.

This is Batman's car. It is from a film. I wonder what it is like to ride inside?

This is another famous car. It is called Chitty Chitty Bang Bang.

This car is the star of a film!

Do you like cars?

Now you know why I like cars! Do you like cars too?

Glossary

break down when something stops working

museum place where interesting objects are displayed for people to look at

petrol fuel for engines

repair to mend something

tyres rubber ring filled with air that covers a wheel and helps it to grip the road

Find out more

Cars: The Essential Guide, Simon Jowett (Dorling Kindersley, 2006)

Getting Around by Car, Cassie Mayer (Heinemann Library, 2006)

Racing Cars, C. Gifford (Usborne Publishing, 2004)

Index

Titles in the *Things I Like* series include:

Hardback   978 0 4311 0960 2

Hardback   978 0 4311 0957 2

Hardback   978 0 4311 0959 6

Hardback   978 0 4311 0953 4

Hardback   978 0 4311 0958 9

Hardback   978 0 4311 0954 1

Hardback   978 0 4311 0956 5

Hardback   978 0 4311 0955 8

Find out about other titles from Heinemann Library on our website www.heinemann.co.uk/library